Wonders Built by Humans

THE GREAT WALL OF CHINA

Sloane Gould

CREATED BY Humans

Published in 2026 by The Rosen Publishing Group, Inc.
2544 Clinton Street, Buffalo, NY 14224

First Edition

Editor: Caitie McAneney
Designer: Rachel Rising

Photo Credits: Cover, feiyuezhangjie/Shutterstock.com; Cover, (series background) Yuliya Chsherbakova/Shutterstock.com; p. 5 Fernando Tatay/Shutterstock.com; p. 6 Jarno Gonzalez Zarraonandia/Shutterstock.com; p. 7 Shane Waldron/Shutterstock.com; p. 9 HiTecherZ/Shutterstock.com; p. 10 Naeemphotographer2/Shutterstock.com; p. 11 ZCOOL HelloRF/Shutterstock.com; p. 13 Xianghong Garrison/Shutterstock.com; p. 14 https://en.m.wikipedia.org/wiki/File:QinShiHuang19century.jpg; p. 15 Andrus Ciprian/Shutterstock.com; p. 16 https://en.m.wikipedia.org/wiki/File:Portrait_assis_de_l%27empereur_Ming_Taizu.jpg; p. 17 Apik/Shutterstock.com; p. 19 DarthAvatar/Shutterstock.com; p. 21 danielcastromaia/Shutterstock.com; p. 22 Michael Linde/Shutterstock.com; p. 23 Hung Chung Chih/Shutterstock.com; p. 25 Collection Maykova/Shutterstock.com; p. 26 Bankoo/Shutterstock.com; p. 27 Maridav/Shutterstock.com; p. 29 cherry-hai/Shutterstock.com.

Cataloging-in-Publication Data

Names: Gould, Sloane.
Title: The Great Wall of China / Sloane Gould.
Description: Buffalo, NY : Created by Humans, an imprint of Rosen Publishing, 2026. | Series: Wonders built by humans | Includes glossary and index.
Identifiers: ISBN 9781534552968 (pbk.) | ISBN 9781534552975 (library bound) | ISBN 9781534552982 (ebook)
Subjects: LCSH: Walls--China--Design and construction--History--Juvenile literature. | Great Wall of China (China)--Juvenile literature. | China--History--To 221 B.C.--Juvenile literature.
Classification: LCC DS793.G67 G685 2026 | DDC 931--dc23

Manufactured in China

CPSIA Compliance Information: Batch #QWCBH26. For Further Information contact Rosen Publishing at 1-800-237-9932.

CONTENTS

HUMANS MADE THAT?!

Some structures on Earth are so amazing that it's hard to believe humans built them. Some things were even built by ancient **civilizations**—without the use of modern materials or **technology**!

From the Great Pyramids of Giza to Machu Picchu, it's clear that ancient civilizations relied on human creativity and **ingenuity**. People designed structures that have stood the test of time. One of the largest human-made structures on Earth is the Great Wall of China. It is proof of the ingenuity of ancient Chinese builders. The existing wall is around 5,500 miles (8,850 km) long. It was once much longer!

The Great Wall is one of the most famous features of China.

WOW!

The Great Wall of China isn't only a human-made structure. The Chinese used existing mountains and rivers as part of the network of walls to keep people out.

A WORLD WONDER

In 2007, the "New Seven Wonders of the World" were chosen. The Great Wall of China was at the top of the list! It's known as one of the largest construction projects ever undertaken. Other world wonders included the ancient Mayan city of Chichén Itzá in Mexico and the ancient Incan city of Machu Picchu in Peru.

The Great Wall became a World Heritage Site in 1987. That means it should be protected at all costs because of its value. It was chosen because of the mastery of its construction, as well as its importance to Chinese history and culture.

The Great Wall is a huge part of Chinese history.

ANCIENT CHINA

Humans have lived in China for at least 40,000 years. About 4,000 years ago, people started forming communities there. The Shang **dynasty** was the first one with written history. It started around 1700 BCE.

The ancient Chinese made great advances in science, writing, technology, and art. Different dynasties rose and fell over the course of thousands of years. Each one **contributed** something to China and many expanded their borders. For example, the Qin dynasty, which lasted only from 221 BCE to 206 BCE, is known for greatly expanding and uniting a network of walls.

WOW!

BCE means "Before Common Era" and CE means "Common Era," which started about 2,026 years ago.

The ancient Chinese invented gunpowder, the compass, and paper for written records.

A BIG CHALLENGE

Today, the Great Wall of China is mostly a tourist attraction. However, when it was built, it had a serious purpose—protection. The ancient Chinese wanted to keep outside armies from invading. However, building such a wall would be a great challenge.

To build a wall that could keep armies out, they would need to make it tall enough to keep people from climbing over. They would need to make it out of materials that would last. They would also need to craft the wall to fit the differing landscapes of the Chinese countryside.

This part of the Great Wall goes over steep mountains!

China's Geography

China's geography made a big difference in how civilization **developed**. The Chinese were mostly isolated, or set apart, from other civilizations. There were dry deserts in the west and north, mountains in the south, and the ocean to the east. The builders of the Great Wall had to work with these different landscapes. Sections of the wall go through mountains, rivers, and deserts. It is built into the landscape, which made it even more effective.

THE OLDEST PARTS

Some parts of the Great Wall were built during a time in Chinese history called the Warring States Period, which lasted from around 475 BCE to 221 BCE. Different states were trying to gain power. Each state wanted to defend itself against others.

Different states started building their own defensive walls to keep their neighbors and other invaders out. A long border wall was started in the Qi state. This wall was mostly made of soil and stones. It made use of river **dikes** and mountainous land to make the area impassable.

WOW!

The oldest parts of the Great Wall of China were built around 2,500 years ago!

This is part of the oldest bit of the Great Wall of China, made thousands of years ago out of earth!

UNITING THE WALLS

The Warring States Period ended when China became united in 220 BCE. The first emperor was Qin Shi Huang. He had a vision. Not only would he unite China—he would also unite the existing walls into one great wall. Instead of keeping neighboring states out, these walls would now mostly be used to protect against northern invaders.

The wall continued to grow. The earliest sections of the wall were made of earth and wood. Some parts were made of brick, granite, or marble. Each emperor advanced the Great Wall, making use of new technology that the Chinese had developed over time.

Qin Shi Huang

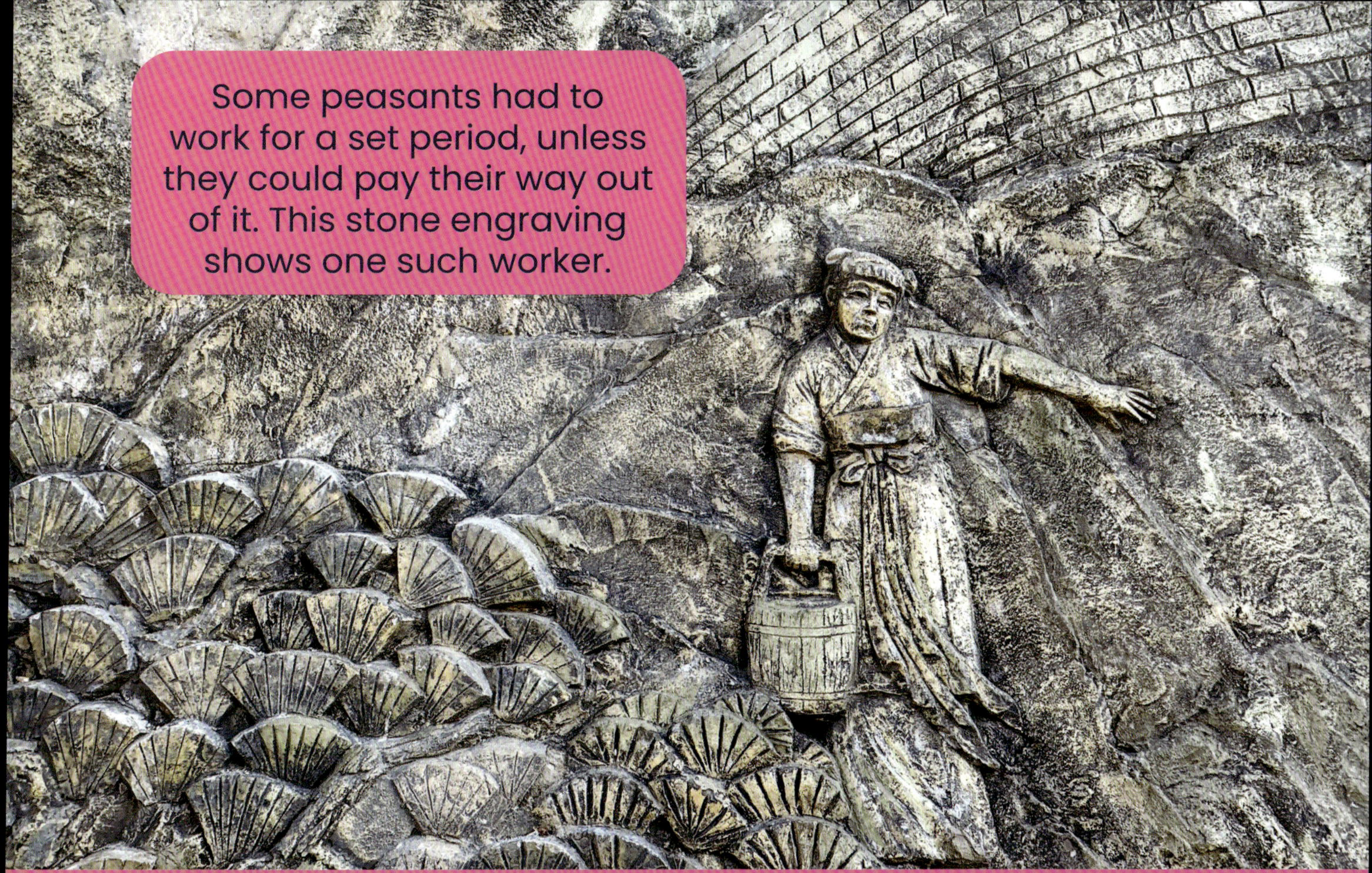

Some peasants had to work for a set period, unless they could pay their way out of it. This stone engraving shows one such worker.

Who Built the Wall?

The Great Wall of China was a massive building project. So who did the building? Some of the work was done by soldiers and peasants. Much of the work was also done by forced laborers, such as criminals or enemies of the emperor. Many people died while working on the Great Wall. They died from poor working conditions, bad weather, illness, and lack of food. It is **rumored** that bodies are buried in the wall, though none have yet been found.

MING MASTERMINDS

Each dynasty made their own special mark on the Great Wall of China. Perhaps the greatest mark was made by the Ming Dynasty, which began in 1368 CE. This dynasty is well known for its contributions to Chinese artwork and **porcelain**. Chinese porcelain was so beautiful that today many people still call anything made of porcelain "china."

These artistic minds also worked to design new areas of the Great Wall of China. In fact, much of what is shown of the Great Wall in pictures is from the Ming dynasty. They designed great watchtowers and platforms.

Zhu Yuanzhang

The Ming dynasty was founded by Zhu Yuanzhang, who was born a commoner.

TERRIFIC TOWERS

When you see pictures of the Great Wall of China, they usually show platforms or towers along the wall. These were designed to help soldiers keep a lookout for invaders.

Some towers provided shelter for soldiers. These towers were usually a rectangular shape, around 50 feet (15 m) tall. They had multiple floors with different **functions**. The first floor was often where soldiers slept and ate. The second floor would have soldiers on duty. They could shoot arrows through holes in the walls. The roof was a watchtower. Since the towers were usually very high on a mountain, soldiers could see all around.

WOW!

The Fairy Tower is a guard tower in the Simatai section of the Great Wall of China. To get to it, visitors climb the "Heavenly Ladder," which is 328 feet (100 m) high!

The Wangjing Tower (also known as the "Watching-the-capital Tower") is so high up, it's said that soldiers could see Beijing 75 miles (120 km) away!

THOUSANDS OF YEARS

The Great Wall of China wasn't built in a day. This huge project took thousands of years, with many **generations** of workers adding to it. It called for creativity and teamwork, and a shared purpose: to protect the people of China. The last sections of the wall were built in the late 1800s.

Much of the Great Wall of China has been lost to time. Its older sections, made of rammed earth, have been harmed by **erosion**. Only about 8 percent of the original wall is intact today. However, the parts people visit—most built during the Ming dynasty—still stand strong.

WOW!

Rammed earth is a building material made from stuffing soil into block molds.

This part of the Great Wall of China stands today because of its strong materials and smart design.

Different Materials

When it comes to standing the test of time, materials matter! The oldest sections of the Great Wall of China were built 2,500 years ago using what the builders had at the time—earth. It's not surprising that these sections have eroded over centuries. Later, stones and bricks were used to build the Great Wall. This is why much of the Ming dynasty wall is still standing today.

THAT'S HUGE!

Just how big is the Great Wall of China? It's not one continuous wall. It's a network of walls and towers. Today, the section that's still standing and in good condition is around 3,400 miles (5,500 km) long. That's wider than the United States from east to west!

The wall was much longer than this, however. It was likely more than 12,400 miles (20,000 km) long. To understand the large scale of this structure, that's almost half the length of the **equator**! More parts of the Great Wall are uncovered as time goes on, so it's likely even bigger than we know.

The wall was built, rebuilt, and added to continuously for around 2,000 years!

WHAT DID IT DO?

The masterminds behind the Great Wall of China meant for it to protect the Chinese people from invasion. Did it work? Some people argue that it didn't work that well. People did attack China, including the Mongols—the enemies to the north that the wall was meant to keep out. In 1211, Mongol troops under Genghis Khan got through the Great Wall and eventually took over China.

However, the wall did keep many invaders from getting into China over thousands of years. It also showed the world the wealth and engineering smarts of the Chinese people.

WOW!

The towers were also used to send news quickly between posts. Soldiers could communicate through fires at night and smoke signals during the day.

This statue shows Genghis Khan (1162 – 1227 CE), the famous warrior and founder of the Mongol Empire.

VISITING THE GREAT WALL

Millions of people visit the Great Wall of China each year. It's one of the most famous landmarks in China, even today. It's a symbol, or a sign, of China's proud history. It's also a symbol of China's long traditions of engineering and architecture.

Today, visitors can walk the steps up to towers, travel along walkways, and look out over the Chinese countryside.

The Great Wall of China is one of the wonders of the world, for good reason. As the largest structure ever built by humans, it amazes all who visit it!

About 10 million people visit the Great Wall of China every year!

YOU CAN DESIGN IT!

Imagine you must create a defensive wall or barrier to protect your community. It needs to be strong enough to withstand natural disasters and attacks from the outside. Time to think like an engineer!

Ask yourself:

- What materials will I use?
- How tall and wide should it be?
- What special features will help with defense?
- How can I make it stand for centuries?

Sketch out some plans for your building on a separate sheet of paper.

Bonus: Share your ideas with friends, or team up to create a wall out of found materials or building bricks.

You can get creative with plastic, interlocking bricks like these.

GLOSSARY

civilization: Organized society with written records and laws.
contribute: To give along with others.
develop: To cause something to become more advanced.
dike: A bank constructed to control or confine water.
dynasty: A succession of rulers of the same line of descent.
equator: An imaginary circle around Earth that's an equal distance from the North Pole and the South Pole.
erosion: The wearing away of earth by wind or water.
function: Something for which a person or thing is specially fitted or used.
generation: A group of individuals born about the same time.
ingenuity: Skill or cleverness that allows people to solve problems and create inventions.
porcelain: A hard, white ceramic material used for plates, bowls, and other wares.
rumor: To tell or spread by rumor, or unproven talk or opinions.
technology: Using science, engineering, and other industries to invent useful tools or to solve problems. Also a machine, piece of equipment, or method created by technology.

FOR MORE INFORMATION

BOOKS

Bradshaw, Eleanor. *20 Things You Didn't Know About the Great Wall of China*. Buffalo, NY: PowerKids Press, 2025.

Lawrence, Blythe. *Great Wall of China*. Lake Elmo, MN: Focus Readers , 2023.

Lynch, Seth. *Ancient China*. Buffalo, NY: Enslow Publishing, 2025.

WEBSITES

The Great Wall of China
education.nationalgeographic.org/resource/great-wall-china
Learn more about the Great Wall of China with National Geographic.

Walk the Great Wall
artsandculture.google.com/project/great-wall-of-china
Take a virtual tour of the Great Wall of China with Google Arts & Culture.

Publisher's note to educators and parents: Our editors have carefully reviewed these websites to ensure that they are suitable for students. Many websites change frequently, however, and we cannot guarantee that a site's future contents will continue to meet our high standards of quality and educational value. Be advised that students should be closely supervised whenever they access the internet.

INDEX